ABSOLUTE BEGINNERS
Keyboard Songbook

To access companion audio, visit:
www.halleonard.com/mylibrary

Enter Code
4830-2393-6366-1271

ISBN 978-0-7119-8127-0

EXCLUSIVELY DISTRIBUTED BY

HAL•LEONARD®

This book © Copyright 2001 by Wise Publications

Visit Hal Leonard Online at
www.halleonard.com

Contact us:
Hal Leonard
7777 West Bluemound Road
Milwaukee, WI 53213
Email: info@halleonard.com

In Europe, contact:
Hal Leonard Europe Limited
42 Wigmore Street
Marylebone, London, W1U 2RN
Email: info@halleonardeurope.com

In Australia, contact:
Hal Leonard Australia Pty. Ltd.
4 Lentara Court
Cheltenham, Victoria, 3192 Australia
Email: info@halleonard.com.au

Arranged by Derek Jones
Music Processed by Paul Ewers
Editing and book layout by Sorcha Armstrong
Cover design by Chloë Alexander
Cover photographs by George Taylor
Audio mastered by Jonas Persson

Contents

Bridge Over Troubled Water

Words & Music by Paul Simon

  Track 1

♩=82

1. When you're

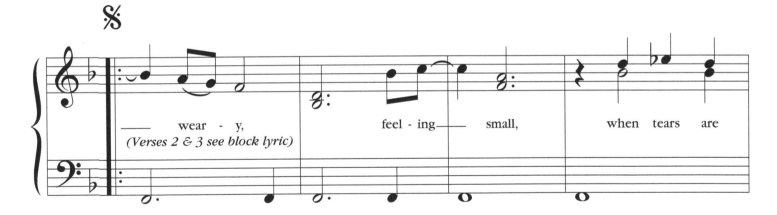

wear - y,
(Verses 2 & 3 see block lyric)
feel - ing small,
when tears are

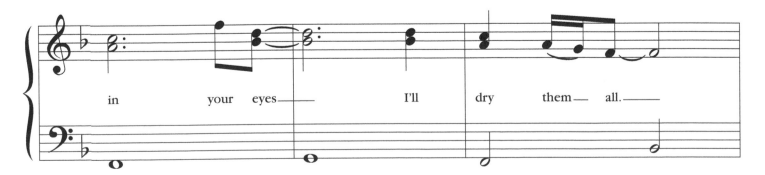

in your eyes
I'll dry them all.

I'm on your side, _____ oh, ___

___ when__ times__ get rough, _____ and friends just

To Coda ⊕

can't be found. Like a bridge ov - er

trou - bled wa - ter, I will lay me down. Like a

1.

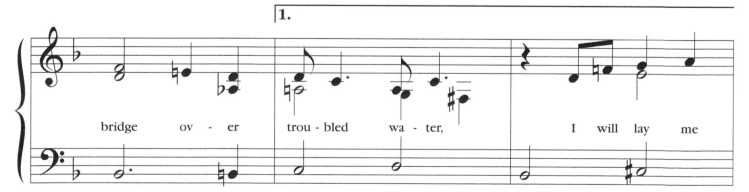

bridge ov - er trou - bled wa - ter, I will lay me

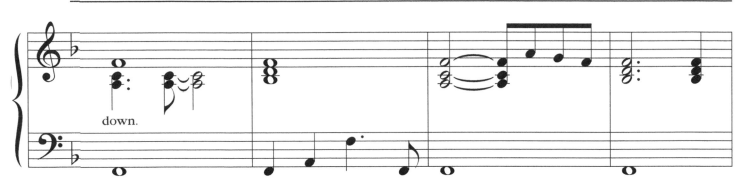

down.

2. When you're   trou - bled   wa - ter,

I will lay me   down.

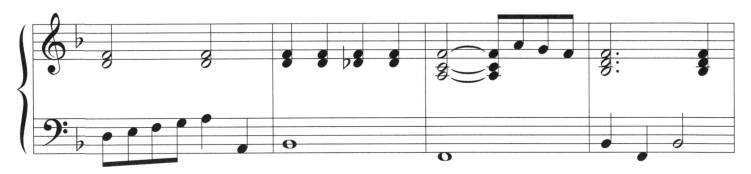

D.%. al Coda

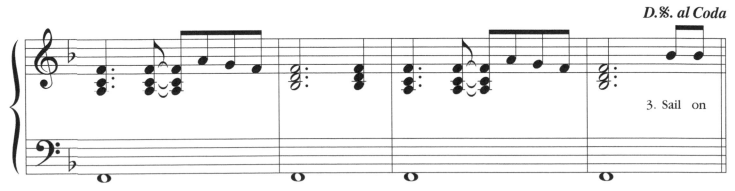

3. Sail on

✠ *Coda*

bridge ov - er trou - bled wa - ter, I will ease your

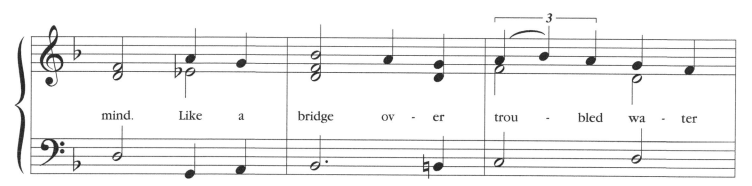

mind. Like a bridge ov - er trou - bled wa - ter

I will ease your mind.

rit.

Verse 2:
When you're down and out
When you're on the street
When evening falls so hard
I will comfort you
I'll take your part
When darkness comes
And pain is all around
Like a bridge over troubled water
I will lay me down
Like a bridge over troubled water
I will lay me down

Verse 3:
Sail on Silver Girl
Sail on by
Your time has come to shine
All your dreams are on their way
See how they shine
If you need a friend
I'm sailing right behind
Like a bridge over troubled water
I will ease your mind
Like a bridge over troubled water
I will ease your mind

Candle In The Wind

Words & Music by Elton John & Bernie Taupin

 Track 2

1. Good - bye Nor - ma Jean.___ Though I nev - er
(Verses 2 & 3 see block lyric)

knew you___ played at all___ you had the grace to

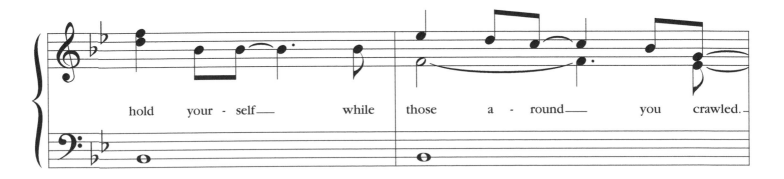

hold your - self___ while those a - round___ you crawled.

They crawled out of the wood - work

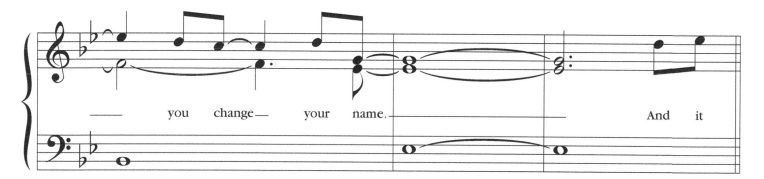

and they whis - pered in - to your brain.

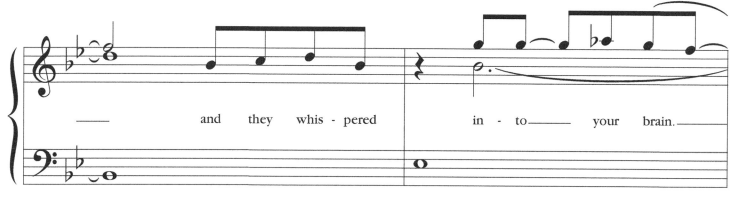

They set you on a tread - mill and they made

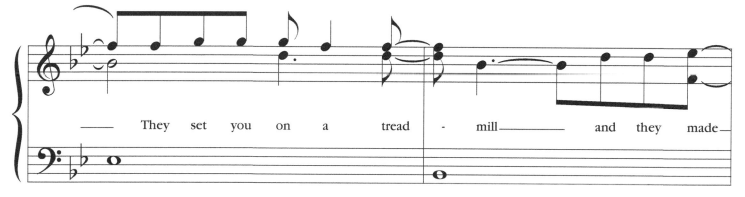

you change your name. And it

seems to me you lived your life like a can - dle in the wind

To Coda

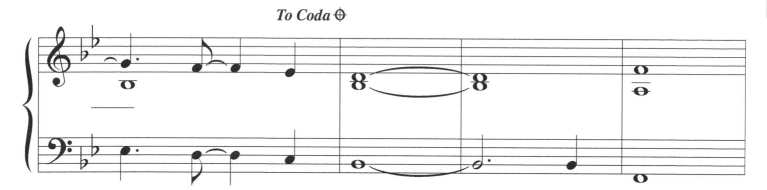

1, 2. *2º D.%. al Coda*

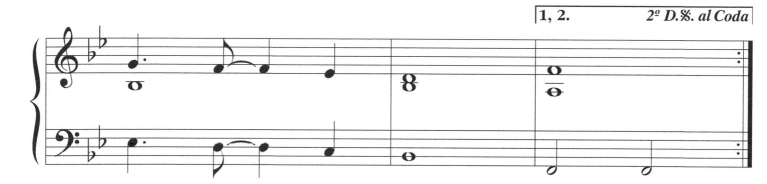

Coda

The can - dle had burned— out long be - fore— your

le - gend ev - er did.———

Verse 2:
Loneliness was tough
The toughest role you ever played
Hollywood created a superstar
And pain was the price you paid
Even when you died
The press still hounded you
All the papers had to say
Was that Marilyn was found in the nude

And it seems to me *etc.*

Verse 3:
Goodbye Norma Jean
Though I never knew you al all
You had the grace to hold yourself
While those around you crawled
Goodbye Norma Jean
From the young man in the twenty second row
Who sees you as something more than sexual
More than just Marilyn Monroe

And it seems to me *etc.*

Eternal Flame

12

Words & Music by Billy Steinberg, Tom Kelly & Susanna Hoffs

 Track 3

1. Close your eyes,
(Verse 2 see block lyric)

give me your hand,— darl - ing. Do you feel— my heart beat - ing, do you un-der-

To Coda

- stand? Do you feel the same,— am I on - ly dream - ing?

1.   2.

Is this burn - ing   an e - ter - nal flame?   Is this burn - ing—

an e-ter-nal flame? Say my name,– sun shines through the rain,—— a whole

life so lone-ly,— and then come and ease– the pain.——

1.

I don't wan - na lose this feel - ing, oh.

2. *D.%. al Coda*

oh.

⊕ *Coda*

dream - ing or is this burn - ing—— an e - ter - nal flame?

—— Close your eyes,—— give me your hand—— dar-ling. Do you feel—— my heart beat-

-ing, do you un - der - stand? Do you feel the same,—— am I on - ly

Repeat to fade

dream - ing? Is this burn - ing—— an e - ter - nal flame?——

Verse 2:
I believe it's meant to be, darling
I want you when you are sleeping
You belong to me
Do you feel the same?
Am I only dreaming?
Is this burning an eternal flame?

Every Breath You Take

Words & Music by Sting

  Track 4

Ev - 'ry breath you— take, ev - 'ry move you—

make, ev - 'ry bond— you break,— ev - 'ry step— you take—

I'll be watch - ing you. Ev - 'ry sin - gle

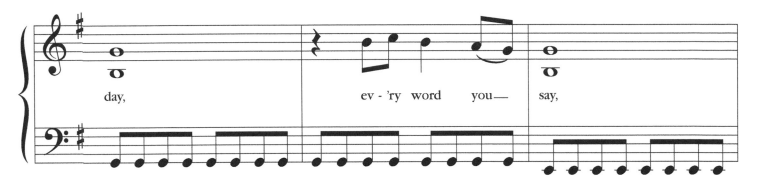

day, ev - 'ry word you— say,

ev - 'ry game— you play,— ev - 'ry night— you say— I'll be watch - ing you.—

Oh, can't you— see

you be - long to me? How my poor heart—

aches ——— with ev - 'ry step— you take.

Ev - 'ry move you— make, ev - 'ry vow you—

break, ev - 'ry smile— you fake,— ev - 'ry claim— you stake.

To Coda ⊕

——— I'll be watch - ing you.—

Since you've gone— I been lost— with - out— a trace, I dreamt at night I can on -

-ly see— your face. I look a-round but it's you I can't— re-place,

I feel so cold and I long for your— em-brace. I keep com - ing ba-

- by, ba - by please.—

D.%. al Coda

Oh, can't you—

⊕ *Coda*

Ev - 'ry move— you make,— ev - 'ry step— you take— I'll be watch - ing you.—

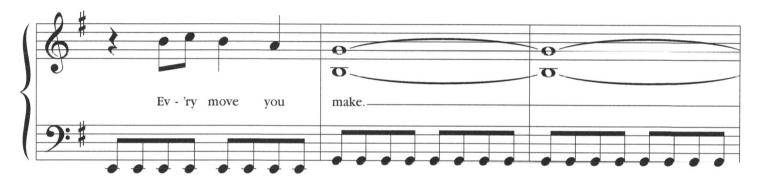

Ev - 'ry move you make.—

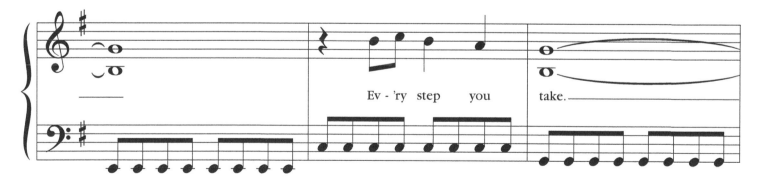

Ev - 'ry step you take.—

I'll be watch - ing you.

Everything I Do (I Do It For You)

Words by Bryan Adams & Robert John Lange. Music by Michael Kamen

Track 5

♩=98

1. Look in - to my eyes,————
(Verse 2 see block lyric)
you will see————

what you mean to———— me. Search your heart,———— search your

soul,———————— and when you find me there you'll search— no more. Don't

tell me it's not worth try-in' for, you can't tell me it's not worth dy-in'

for._____ You know it's true,_____ ev-'ry-thing I

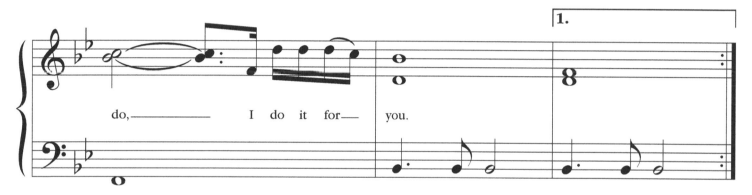

do,_____ I do it for__ you.

1.

8

2.

There's no love_____ like your love_____ and no

oth - er could give more_____ love. There's no - where_____ un - less

you're— there,—— all the time,———— all the way,— yeah.——

1.　　　　　　　　　　　　　　　　　**2.**

Oh,　you can't

tell　me　it's not　worth　try - in'　for,　　　　I　can't

help———　it,　there's no - thin' I　want　more.———— Yeah, I　would

Verse 2:
Look into my heart, you will find
There's nothing there to hide
Take me as I am, take my life
I would give it all I would sacrifice

Don't tell me it's not worth fighting for
I can't help it there's nothing I want more
You know it's true
Everything I do, I do it for you.

Hey Jude

Words & Music by John Lennon & Paul McCartney

Track 6

♩=76

1. Hey Jude, _____ don't make it bad, take a

sad song _____ and make it bet - ter. _____ Re -

- mem - ber to let her in - to your heart. Then you can start ____

____ to make it ____ bet - ter. 2. Hey

Jude,————— don't be a - fraid, you were made to——— go out and
(Verse 3 see block lyric)

get her.——— The min - ute you let her un - der your

skin, then you be - gin——— to make it——— bet - ter.

And a - ny time—— you feel the pain,—— hey Jude,—— re - frain,—

——— don't car - ry the world—— up - on——— your shoul - ders.———

For well you know— that it's a fool— who plays— it cool— by mak - ing his world

—— a lit - tle cold - er.—— Na na na na na na na na

1.

na. 3. Hey—

2.

Hey—

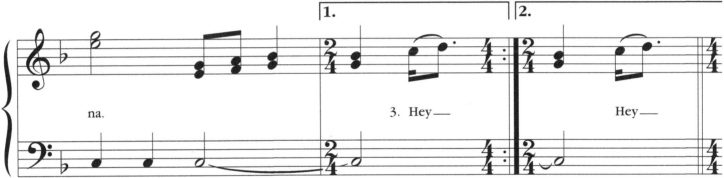

Jude,————— don't make it bad, take a

sad song—— and make it bet - ter.—— Re -

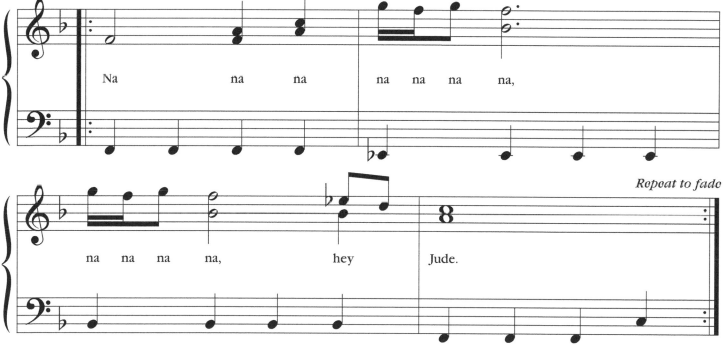

Verse 3:

Hey Jude, don't let me down
You have found her, now go and get her
Remember to let her into your heart
Then you can start to make it better
So let it out and let it in
Hey Jude, begin, you're waiting for someone to perform with
And don't you know that it's just you
Hey Jude, you'll do, the movement you need is on your shoulder

Na na na na na na *etc.*

Imagine

Words & Music by John Lennon

 Track 7

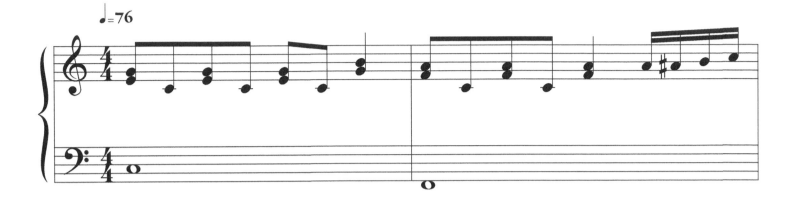

1. I - ma - gine there's no hea - ven,

it's ea - sy if you try.

No hell_____ be - low us,

a - bove us on - ly sky.

I - ma - gine all the peo - ple_____

liv - ing for to - day._____ A - ha._____

2. I - ma - gine there's no coun - tries,
(Verse 3 see block lyric)

it is - n't hard to do.

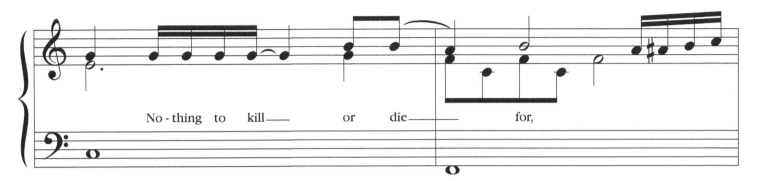

No - thing to kill—— or die—— for,

no re - li - gion too.——

I - ma - gine all the peo - ple——

liv - ing life in peace.—— A - ha——

You may say I'm a dream - er,

but I'm not the on - ly one.

I hope some day you'll join us,

and the world will live as one. live as one.

Verse 2:

Imagine no possessions
I wonder if you can
No need for greed or hunger
A brotherhood of man
Imagine all the people
Sharing all the world

You may say I'm a dreamer *etc.*

Money Money Money

Words & Music by Benny Andersson & Björn Ulvaeus

 Track 8

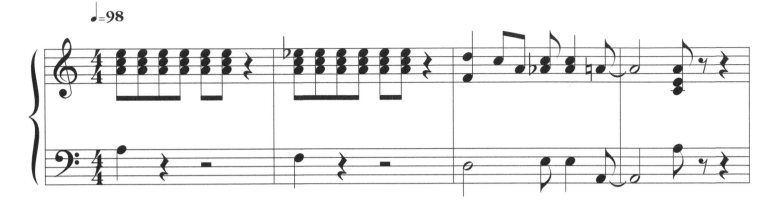

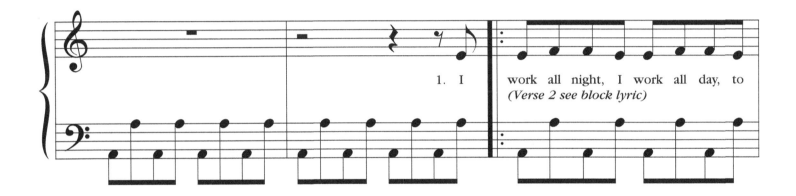

1. I work all night, I work all day, to
(Verse 2 see block lyric)

pay the bills I have to pay,— ain't it sad?— And

still there nev- er seems to be a sin- gle pen- ny left for me,— that's too bad.

In my dreams— I have a plan,— if I got me a

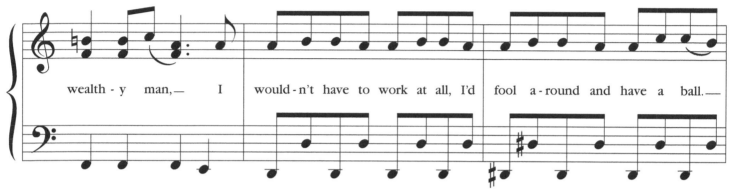

wealth - y man,— I would - n't have to work at all, I'd fool a - round and have a ball.—

Mo - ney, mo - ney, mo - ney,

must be fun - ny, in the rich man's world.— Mo - ney, mo - ney, mo - ney,

al - ways sun - ny, in the rich man's world.— A - ha,—

a - ha. _____ All the things I could do _____ if I

had a lit - tle mo - ney, it's a rich man's world. _____

1.

It's a rich man's world. _____ 2. A

2.

Mo - ney, mo - ney, mo - ney, al - ways sun - ny,

in the rich man's world. _____ Mo - ney, mo - ney, mo - ney,

al - ways sun - ny, in the rich man's world.___ A - ha,—

— a - ha.___ All the things I could do— if I

had a lit - tle mo - ney, it's a rich man's world.—

Verse 2:

A man like that is hard to find but I can't get him off my mind

Ain't it sad

And if he happens to be free I bet he wouldn't fancy me

That's too bad

So I must leave, I'll have to go

To Las Vegas or Monaco

And win a fortune in a game, my life will never be the same

Mull Of Kintyre

Words & Music by Paul McCartney & Denny Laine

 Track 9

Mull of Kin - tyre, oh, mist roll - ing in from— the

sea, my de - sire is al - ways to be here, oh,

Mull of Kin - tyre.

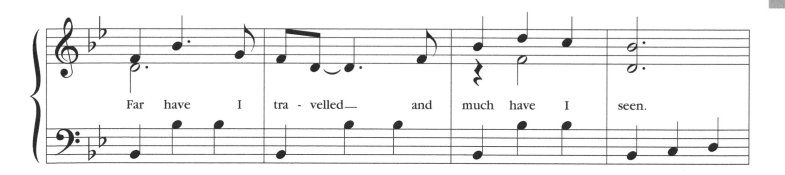

Far have I tra - velled— and much have I seen.

Dark dis - tant moun - tains— with val - leys of green.

Past paint - ed des - erts— the sun - set's on fire as he car -

- ries me home— to the Mull of Kin - tyre.

Mull of Kin - tyre, oh, mist roll - ing in from— the

Sweep through the wea - ther— like deer in the glen,

car - ry me back to the days I knew then.

Nights when we sang like a hea - ven - ly choir of the

D.%. al Coda

life and the times of the Mull of Kin - tyre.—

⊕ *Coda*

Audio Track Listing

Track 1   **Bridge Over Troubled Water**

(Simon)
Pattern Music

Track 2   **Candle In The Wind**

(John/Taupin)
Universal/Dick James Music Limited

Track 3   **Eternal Flame**

(Steinberg/Kelly/Hoffs)
Sony/ATV Music Publishing (UK) Limited/
Universal Music Publishing Limited

Track 4   **Every Breath You Take**

(Sting)
Magnetic Publishing Limited/EMI Music Publishing Limited

Track 5   **Everything I Do (I Do It For You)**

(Adams/Lange/Kamen)
Universal/MCA Music Limited/Rondor Music (London) Limited/
Zomba Music Publishers Limited

Track 6   **Hey Jude**

(Lennon/McCartney)
Northern Songs/Sony/ATV Music Publishing (UK) Limited

Track 7   **Imagine**

(Lennon)
Lenono Music

Track 8   **Money Money Money**

(Andersson/Ulvaeus)
Bocu Music Limited

Track 9   **Mull Of Kintyre**

(McCartney/Laine)
MPL Communications Limited